What I Did on My Summer Vacation

Kids' Favorite Funny Summer Vacation Poems

What I Did on My Summer Vacation

Kids' Favorite Funny Summer Vacation Poems

Edited by

Bruce Lansky

Illustrated by

Stephen Carpenter

Ⓜ Meadowbrook Press

Distributed by Simon & Schuster
New York

Library of Congress Cataloging-in-Publication Data

What I did on my summer vacation : kids' favorite funny poems about summer
vacation / edited by Bruce Lansky ; illustrated by Stephen Carpenter.
   p. cm.
 ISBN-10: 0-88166-539-8 (Meadowbrook Press); 1-4169-7047-9 (Simon & Schuster)
 ISBN-13: 978-0-88166-539-0 (Meadowbrook Press); 978-1-4169-7047-7 (Simon & Schuster)
 1. Summer--Juvenile poetry. 2. Children's poetry, American. 3. Vacations--Juvenile poetry.
 4. Humorous poetry, American. I. Lansky, Bruce. II. Carpenter, Stephen, ill.
 PS591.S3W46 2009
 811'.608033--dc22
                              2008042864

Coordinating Editor and Copyeditor: Angela Wiechmann
Editorial Assistant and Proofreader: Alicia Ester
Production Manager: Paul Woods
Graphic Design Manager: Tamara Peterson
Illustrations and Cover Art: Stephen Carpenter

Published by Meadowbrook Press
5451 Smetana Drive
Minnetonka, Minnesota 55343

www.meadowbrookpress.com

BOOK TRADE DISTRIBUTION by Simon and Schuster,
a division of Simon and Schuster, Inc.
1230 Avenue of the Americas
New York, New York 10020

14 13 12 11 10 09   10 9 8 7 6 5 4 3 2 1

Printed in the United States of America

Acknowledgments

Many thanks to the following teachers and their
students who tested poems for this anthology:

Diane Clapp, Lincoln Elementary, Fairbault, MN
Niki Danou, Groveland Elementary, Minnetonka, MN
Jeremy Engebretson, Groveland Elementary, Minnetonka, MN
Marianne Gately, McCarthy Elementary, Framingham, MA
Kathy Kenney-Marshall, McCarthy Elementary, Framingham, MA
Theresa Lifer, Butler Elementary, Butler, OH
Mary Jensen, East Elementary, New Richmond, WI
Carolyn Larsen, Rum River Elementary, Andover, MN
Carol Larson, Rum River Elementary, Andover, MN
Carmen Markgren, East Elementary, New Richmond, WI
Jenny Myer, East Elementary, New Richmond, WI
John Pundsack, East Elementary, New Richmond, WI
Connie Roetzer, East Elementary, New Richmond, WI
Suzanne Storbeck, Holy Name School, Wayzata, MN

Contents

Introduction

I love summer, don't you? Every spring, I can hardly wait for summer to begin. And once it begins, I hope it will never end. But end it must, so on the first day of school, everyone wants to know what you did on your summer vacation.

During summer vacation, you get to do all of your favorite things: cook hot dogs over a campfire (while being eaten alive by mosquitoes); relax with a book poolside (while kids spray you with water guns and cannonballs); play baseball (with a pitcher who can't throw the ball over the plate); take a road trip to visit relatives who live near the Grand Canyon, Disney World, or Niagara Falls (without actually getting to see those attractions); and ride on a scary roller coaster (that turns you and your tummy topsy-turvy).

This is the funniest collection of summer vacation adventures ever published. I hope your own summer adventures are half as entertaining as the ones in this book. (Just for fun, write a story or poem about what you did over summer vacation and entertain your classmates and teacher with it.)

Happy summer,

Bruce Lansky

My Summer Vacation

I have a special talent that I learned right here at school.
My friends all asked to see me try. They said, "Come on, it's cool!"
So I unlocked my locker's door and flung it open wide.
I said, "For your amusement, I will close myself inside."

I squished and squeezed and twisted limbs while trying to get in.
My nose was crushed by smelly shoes. Some gum was on my chin.
With moldy cupcakes underfoot, a coat hook in my ear,
I used my toe to close the door. My friends began to cheer.

But then I heard the school bell ring. My friends yelled, "Yay, we're done!"
I panicked as I figured out that summer had begun.
I tried to open up the door, but somehow it had locked.
So I began to kick and scream. I shouted and I knocked.

But it was all of little use 'cause everyone was gone.
I tried to bust my locker door, but didn't have the brawn.
Most kids will spend their summer playing games like tag or soccer,
but not poor me—I'll spend my summer trapped inside my locker.

Robert Pottle

The Teachers Jumped Out of the Windows

(sing to the tune of "My Bonnie")

The teachers jumped out of the windows.
The principal ran for the door.
The nurse and librarian bolted.
They're not coming back anymore.

The counselor, hollering madly,
escaped out the door of the gym.
The coach and custodian shouted
and ran out the door after him.

Chorus
Oh my! Goodbye!
They're not coming back anymore, no more.
How fun! They've run!
They're not coming back anymore.

The lunch ladies threw up their ladles,
then fled from the kitchen in haste,
and all of the students looked puzzled
as staff members scurried and raced.

We'd never seen anything like it.
But still, it was pretty darned cool
to see all the staff so excited
to leave on the last day of school.

Chorus
Oh my! Goodbye!
They're not coming back anymore, no more.
How fun! They've run!
They're not coming back anymore.

Kenn Nesbitt

The Last Day of School

Summer vacation is starting today.
The teachers are shouting out, "Hip, hip, hooray!"
Our grumpy old principal grins ear to ear
and runs down the hall shouting, "Summer is here!"
The buses come early. (They're usually late.)
The teachers say, "Hurry up! Pack up! Don't wait!"
The school bell is ringing. There's no time to chat.
The whole school is emptied in one second flat.
Everyone's happy. Our spirits are flying.
Except for our parents—they're sulking and crying.

Robert Pottle

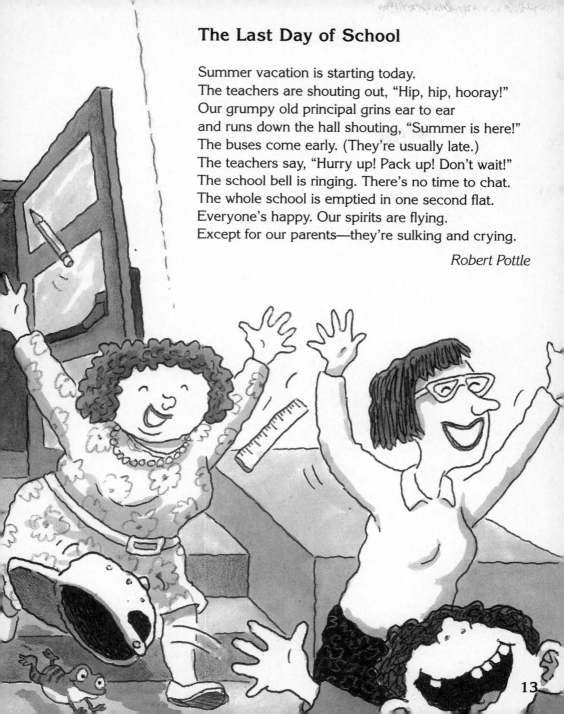

Summer Blues

At last, at last, it's summertime!
The school is closed up tight.
No mean and scary teachers.
No more spelling words to write.
No quizzes and no horrid tests.
No science, reading, math.
No unexciting homework,
and no boring nightly bath.
No waking at the crack of dawn.
No bedtime rules to break.
No faking flu or chickenpox
or dreadful bellyache.
No wearing clothes I really hate—
just bathing suits and shorts
to wear while hunting tons of frogs
that give me tons of warts.
It's time to suck on Popsicles.
It's time for lemonade.
It's time to go to beaches
and then play in the arcade.

It's time for building awesome forts.
It's time for hide-and-seek.
It's time for going barefoot
while you're fishing in the creek.
It's time to go to bed real late
with dirt beneath my nails
from hunting salamanders, bugs,
and slimy, creeping snails.
I dream of all the stuff I'll find
while drifting off to sleep:
a really ancient arrowhead,
a pile of gold to keep!
But as I eat my breakfast
on my first full day of fun,
my mom said, "Summer
   reading's here—
no playing till it's done."
So now the salamanders roam.
No fort, no arrowhead.
Just tons of books and me alone,
left moping on my bed.

Kathy Kenney-Marshall

15

I Love Summer—
Except...

I love all the fun
that summertime brings—
excepting, of course
just one or two things:
Except for the ticks
and spiders and bees.
Except for the pollen
from grasses and trees.
Except for the sunburn
and rashes from heat,
and sidewalks so hot
they burn up your feet.

Except for sour grapes
and melons with seeds,
and slithery snakes
that hide in the weeds.
Except for mosquitoes
that suck on your skin,
and all of the flies
that let themselves in.
Except for the warm nights
when I sleep in a cot.
Except for the weather
that's humid and hot.
Except for the smog,
the dust, and the grime...

But other than that,
I love summertime.

Janice Kuharski

Out of Sight

A trampoline or pogo stick:
they both are fun, so take your pick.
But never try them both at once.
Samantha did, that silly dunce.
And now her parents fret and frown
and hope someday she'll come back down.

Eric Ode

Street Pizza

When the sticky summer heat-za
makes your sidewalk and your street-za
burn the bottoms of your feet-za,
take some flour made of wheat-za,
add some eggs, and slowly beat-za
till your dough is quite complete-za.
Then you squish onto the street-za,
add a sauce that's red and sweet-za
and some mushrooms and some meat-za.
When your brother wants to eat-za,
let him come and take a seat-za
for a very special treat-za.
It's a piece o' street-za pizza!

Eric Ode

Who Needs Lemons?

My mother peeked inside the fridge,
and then I saw her shrug.
"Now, where's the milk?" I heard her ask.
"I know I bought a jug."

"I sold it to the neighbor kids
for fifty cents a cup.
They really wanted lemonade,
but still, they drank it up."

"You sold our milk?" my mother screamed.
"That's totally absurd!"
"But Mom, it said right on the front,
Must sell by August 3rd."

Linda Knaus

Dirty Socks

When I went on a camping trip
my father yelled, "PU!
Your socks smell worse than
   rotten eggs
and worse than doggy poo."

"You'd better take them off," he said,
"and wash them in the lake."
It wasn't long before I knew
he'd made a big mistake.

The water changed from clear
   to mud.
Then fumes began to rise.
And soon a cloud of air pollution
covered up the skies.

When bullfrogs started croaking
and ducks began to quack,
some campers started chanting,
"We want our clean lake back!"

I've got a couple of dirty socks.
I'm in an awful bind.
I guess I'll have to bury them.
I hope the worms don't mind.

Bruce Lansky

The Princess of the Monkey Bars

I'm the Princess of the Monkey Bars.
I'm always upside down.
I smile while I am hanging;
don't mistake it for a frown.

My ponytails are dangling.
My crown's clipped to my head.
I've been hanging for so long,
my face is turning red.

I choose who climbs the monkey bars.
I'm strict but always fair.
But still some kids make fun of me
while others simply stare.

I'm embarrassed to admit it,
but I really must confess
that the Princess of the Monkey Bars
should not have worn a dress.

Robert Pottle

Deep-Sea Squeeze

I'm wrapped from top to bottom
in an octopus embrace
with seven arms around my waist
and one across my face.

It all began this morning
with a scuba diving trip.
I found the creature wedged beneath
a sunken pirate ship.

So, carefully, I dug him free.
He offered no objection
but covered me in tentacles
with octopus affection.

It seems I've made a friend today,
but this I'd like to know:
How do you say, in octopus,
"You're welcome. Please let go"?

Eric Ode

27

Fishing with Jordan

"We're going on a fishing trip,"
my father said one morning.
"So pack your gear, we're out of here—
but let me give a warning.

"You might not like the thought of it,
but still this much is true:
The boat has room enough for three,
so Jordan's coming, too."

I knew to moan or gripe or groan
would be a big mistake.
So, soon enough, the three of us
were floating on the lake.

The squirmy worms we used for bait—
they made me kind of queasy.
But Jordan took my worm and hook
and showed me it was easy.

I wouldn't touch the fish I caught,
so Jordan grabbed the tail
and quickly cleaned and cut him up
and threw him in the pail.

Now, sometimes Jordan's in the way,
but this time I was wrong.
In fact, I'm kind of glad
my little sister came along.

Eric Ode

The Top of My Hot Dog
(sing to the tune of "On Top Of Old Smoky")

The top of my hot dog
is no longer bare.
It now has a topping
I didn't want there.

I ordered my hot dog.
I ordered it plain,
without any toppings.
I ordered in vain.

Well, I started eating,
then looked up in the air.
A seagull flew toward me
and gave me a scare.

I covered my hot dog
a second too late.
What fell from that seagull's
too gross to relate.

The top of my hot dog
is no longer bare.
It now has a topping
a seagull put there.

Robert Pottle

Take Me Out of the Ball Game
(sing to the tune of "Take Me Out to the Ball Game")

Take me out of the ball game.
Take me off of the field.
This game has lasted for way too long.
Now I'm singing a desperate song
'cause I have to go to the bathroom.
I think that sports drink's to blame.
And I hope that I don't wet my pants
in this long ball game.

Robert Pottle

31

Skeeter-Man Jack

When pesky mosquitoes
bite Skeeter-Man Jack,
he doesn't complain.
He just bites them right back.

He couldn't care less
if they're covered with mud
or pumped up and plump
til they're bursting with blood.

He bites them despite
them being sticky with sap
or missing a wing
from escaping a slap.

He might find one buzzing
around in his ear,
then nibble it nimbly
cause he's got no fear.

The truth of the matter:
He likes how they taste
and thinks it's a shame
if a bug goes to waste.

So leave him alone
while he's chewin' and lickin.'
He savors the flavor—
they taste just like chicken.

Neal Levin

Itches

I'm covered in calamine lotion
from forehead on down to my feeters
to stop me from scratching the itches
of hundreds of bites from mosqueeters.

My arms and my legs are so itchy,
they feel like they're starting to smoke.
I guess that I got that from playing
in patches of red poison oak.

As if it could not be more painful,
my stomach is rashy and hivey,
my back and my sides are all blotchy
from wandering through poison ivy.

Despite that I'm itching like crazy,
I hardly can wait until when
my itches and rashes are better,
so I can go camping again.

Kenn Nesbitt

Abusement Park

We went to an amusement park,
my family and I.
We rode on rides so scary,
I expected I would die.

We rode a roller coaster
called the Homicidal Comet.
It had so many loop-de-loops
it nearly made us vomit.
We rode the Crazed Tornado,
and it jerked us hard and quick.
If it were any longer,
we would certainly be sick.

We rode the Psycho Octopus,
which packed a nasty punch.
I think we're pretty lucky
that we didn't lose our lunch.

Kenn Nesbitt

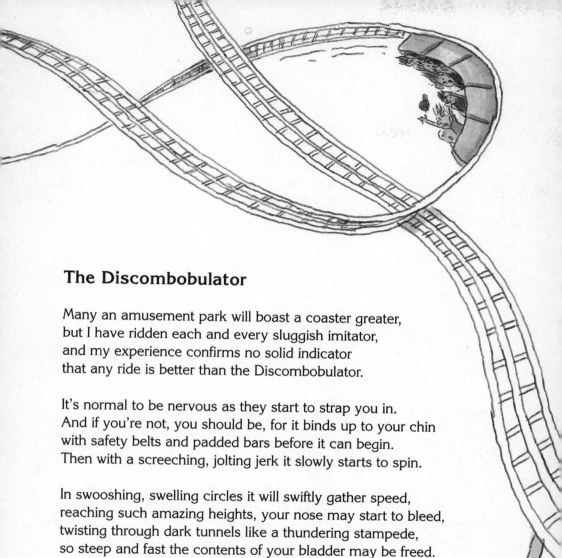

The Discombobulator

Many an amusement park will boast a coaster greater,
but I have ridden each and every sluggish imitator,
and my experience confirms no solid indicator
that any ride is better than the Discombobulator.

It's normal to be nervous as they start to strap you in.
And if you're not, you should be, for it binds up to your chin
with safety belts and padded bars before it can begin.
Then with a screeching, jolting jerk it slowly starts to spin.

In swooshing, swelling circles it will swiftly gather speed,
reaching such amazing heights, your nose may start to bleed,
twisting through dark tunnels like a thundering stampede,
so steep and fast the contents of your bladder may be freed.

Down and down a drop that hurls you under the equator,
your stomach hovers at the top, resigned to join you later.
Your cheeks blow back into your ears; you need a respirator.
But, oh, such pride if you survive the Discombobulator!

Lynne Hockley

Letter from Camp

Dear Mom and Dad,
I hate this camp.
The cabin leaks.
My bed is damp.

The food is gross.
Mosquitoes bite.
The girls are such
an awful sight.

The days are hot.
At night I freeze.
My underwear
is in the trees.

My counselor's mean.
It's so uncool.
But still, I'm glad
I'm not in school.

Neal Levin

Hooray for Summer Camp!

Hooray! I'm off to summer camp,
where life is cold and dark and damp.
Well, maybe once a week it's not,
but then it's scorchy-torchy hot.

At camp we never laugh or play.
The food is overcooked and gray.
The counselors are huge and mean.
Our shower stalls are gross and green.

Our cabins stink from shoes and skunks,
and hungry bedbugs share our bunks.
The flies are big as fighter planes;
they suck your blood and then your brains.

We're not allowed to make a sound,
so all we do is stand around
and swat and itch and never rest.
Compared to home, my camp's the best!

Ted Scheu

39

Christmas in July

If Christmas happened in July, we wouldn't have to freeze.
We'd get our shopping done when it was eighty-five degrees.

There'd be a lot of picnics and there'd be a lot of noise.
Besides parades and fireworks, we'd also get new toys.

So what if Santa had no snow to land in with his sleigh?
He'd drive the coolest SUV and jingle all the way.

But Christmas in July would be a horrible mistake,
'cause when December rolled around, there'd be no Christmas break.

Neal Levin

Family Reunion

For our family reunion in the middle of July,
my mother's sister Helen baked an elderberry pie.
My father's sister Gladys brought the burgers and the ribs.
His other sister, Bobbie, brought the napkins and the bibs.

My uncle Bernie's wife prepared a bucket full of wings.
My cousin Matthew's mother made a salad fit for kings.
And Grandma's daughter Lily and her sister Betty Lou
brought sweet-potato-beet-tomato-hot-tamale stew.

My grandpa's daughter Anna brought zucchini in a pot.
She cooked it for a week, but it was never really hot.
The coleslaw and potato salad both were from Bernice.
You probably don't know her; she's my grandma's sister's niece.

My uncle's dear wife, Rhoda, brought the soda and the punch.
She also brought antacid for her husband after lunch.
Before we started eating, all the ladies did a dance.
I'm glad they all attended—what's a picnic without aunts?

Neal Levin

The Colorful Pool Party

Unhappy with silvery gray on her head,
my auntie decided to dye her hair red—
then dove in our pool, not knowing chlorine
would change Auntie's hair to a frog-colored green.

Helen Ksypka

Diving for Lincoln

We dive for pennies in our pool.
It's all we do since we left school.
I throw them in and say, "Here goes—
I hope Abe Lincoln holds his nose!"

Matthew Fredericks

45

Growing Gardens

I tried to grow a flower bed,
but every single flower's dead.
The first mistake I think I made
was feeding roses lemonade.
I've demonstrated I'm too dumb
to keep alive chrysanthemum.
Perhaps I'm just a little lazy—
I can't even grow a daisy.
I will bet I'd even kill
a violet or a daffodil.

I tried some vegetables instead.
You got it right—the plants are dead.
No squash, zucchini, red tomatoes.
No radishes, no sweet potatoes.
A new idea is in my head:
To grow the perfect crop instead.
But there aren't stores that sell
   the seeds
to grow a garden full of weeds.

Kathy Kenney-Marshall

Steps to Having a Barbecue

First, Dad gets the tools he'll need
and lays them in a row.
Next, he puts his apron on—
a sign he's set to go.

He cleans the surface of the grill
with his wire brush.
He takes his time because my dad
is seldom in a rush.

Mom brings the meat out on a plate
and sets it near at hand.
Dad slathers on the barbecue—
his special homemade brand.

I gather all the other stuff,
like mustard, rolls, and chips,
and paper plates and napkins to
wipe all the messy drips.

And now the moment has arrived
when Dad will light his grill.
He pours the charcoal in just so
and heaps it in a hill.

We've almost reached the final step.
His work is nearly done.
Dad lights the match—Mom grabs the phone
for calling 911.

Mary Jane Mitchell

Fast Food

When it comes to barbecue,
my uncle Len's the boss.
He doesn't follow recipes,
but mixes his own sauce.

He won't tell the ingredients,
not even to my aunt.
When others try to equal it,
they soon find out they can't.

Spicy hot and sugary,
it's even good on fish.
In fact, my uncle Lennie claims
it sweetens *any* dish.

I thought I'd put it to the test
on good old Cousin Herm.
When nobody was looking
I spread sauce upon a worm.

I spooned the worm onto his plate
and told him it was ready.
He watched it crawl away and said,
"I don't eat live spaghetti."

Timothy Tocher

49

Take a Hike

My parents groove on hiking.
It's what we always do.
When we are on vacation,
we're off to find a view.

They bring back lots of photos
of views they think are neat.
I bring back poison ivy
and blisters on my feet.

Mary Jane Mitchell

Super Summer Sale

Come shop at the sale of the year!
There's furniture, clothing, and gear.
If you need some stuff,
there's more than enough.
You'll love what we're offering here.

My brother's guitar is for sale,
a jacket he bought through the mail,
his swimsuit and flippers,
his bathrobe and slippers,
the backpack he wears on the trail.

My brother's new skateboard and ramp,
his radio, dresser, and lamp.
No offer's too low.
It all has to go.
Tomorrow he comes home from camp.

Eric Ode

Garage Sale

Most every summer Mom works hard,
beginning right at dawn,
by putting things she doesn't want
for sale out on the lawn.

Those bargain prices drive folks nuts.
This year they went too far.
One lady bought our front porch steps.
Another bought our car.

And then it got ridiculous,
so that's when I got mad.
"Hey, lady! Some things aren't for sale—
now please put down my dad!"

Linda Knaus

Swimming Lessons

Got my bathing suit and vest.
Got my kickboard. It's the best.
Got my flippers on my toes.
Got my plugs for ears and nose.
Got my kiddie water wings.
Got my rubber floaty things.
Got my wetsuit on, I do.
Got my life preserver, too.
Got my goggles, got my cap.
Got my underwater map.
Got my whistle if I'm stuck.
Got my lucky rubber duck.
Got my snorkel, got my mask.
Got my lifeboat (please don't ask).
Got a lifeguard, fit and trim.
Got no need to learn to swim.

Neal Levin

Cannonball

The lifeguard won't let me go back in the pool.
He tells me I've broken his number one rule.
He didn't approve of my summertime smash—
The Sultan of Soakers, the cannonball splash.

The cannonball calls for an uncommon flair;
with legs tucked beneath me, I soared through the air.
With a splash that would make me the talk of the school,
I think that I just about emptied the pool.

I splashed Mr. Meese and his silly new hat.
I splashed Mrs. Simpkins, who called me a brat.
I splashed Suzy Smith from her head to her feet
and even the lifeguard, whose whistle went *tweet!*

So now here I sit in the heat of the day.
No running. No splashing. And no way to play.
My friends are all swimming and staying real cool,
but the lifeguard won't let me go back in the pool.

Dave Crawley

Driving Our Parents
(A Summer Vacation Road Trip Poem for Two Sweet Voices)

He's pinching my fingers! ....*She's pulling my hair!*

He's laughing too loudly! ....*She's breathing my air!*

He's touching my shoulder! ....*She's stomping my shoes!*

He's punching my muscles!......................*She's bashing my bruise!*

My brother's a doofus! ....*My sister's a freak!*

We're driving to Grandma's ....*to stay for a week!*

We're doing our best................................*to be absolute pains!*

We're driving our parents...........................*clear out of their brains!*

Ted Scheu

58

Dad, Are We There Yet?

"Dad, are we there yet?"
"What's taking so long?"
"How come we're not moving?"
"Has something gone wrong?"

"I'm carsick." "I'm nauseous."
"My underwear's wet."
"I'm dizzy." "I'm fainting."
"My tummy's upset."

"Hey, Mom, crack the window."
"I'm sweating like mad."
"I'm thirsty." "I'm hungry."
"My head's hurting bad."

"My seat belt's too binding."
"Watch out, there's a cop!"
"I'm starting to vomit."
"We might need a mop."

"People are honking."
"They're starting to pass."
"I guess you forgot, Dad,
to fill up with gas."

Paul Orshoski

Summer at Grandma's House

My parents, they sent me to Grandma's this summer.
They said it would do me some good.
They hoped I'd return at the end of vacation
behaving the way that I should.

My grandma is someone I love without measure,
but she can be terribly strict.
And so, when my folks chose a summertime sitter,
my grandma's the person they picked.

They packed me a suitcase and bought me a ticket.
My train left the station at four.
And sure as my grandma eats oatmeal for breakfast,
I quickly arrived at her door.

I thought I'd be scolded and taught about manners
and told I am sloppily dressed.
But staying at Grandmother's house for the summer
is nothing like I would have guessed.

I grunt and I belch and I don't take a shower.
I act like a wild chimpanzee.
I'm living on cookies and ice cream and pizza
and watching late-late night TV.

My parents, they never told Grams I was coming.
I guess that is perfectly plain.
And Grandma, it seems, never told Mom and Dad
she was spending the summer in Spain.

Eric Ode

We Went to New York City

We went to New York City,
but we never saw Times Square.
We just saw Uncle Henry
and played lots of solitaire.

We drove up to Niagara,
but we never saw the Falls.
We stayed in Cousin Ernie's house.
I almost climbed the walls!

We traveled down to Florida
to see our Auntie Sue.
We never went to Disney World
like other people do.

We drove to Arizona
just to see Great-Grandpa Clark.
I wish we'd had the time to see
Grand Canyon National Park.

HOLLYWOOD

And then we took a little trip
to Washington DC.
We didn't see the White House
'cause we stayed with Aunt Marie.

We even went to California
several years ago.
We never got to Hollywood,
but we saw Grandma Flo.

So why'd we stay with relatives
no matter where we went?
It's 'cause my daddy is so cheap—
he will not spend a cent.

Pat Dodds

Harvey's RV

Harvey had the coolest RV anyone had seen.
Longer—even sleeker—than a fancy limousine.
Inside there was a room for games, where Harvey sat and played.
He never had to clean it, for they had a live-in maid.

The couch was soft and comfy, and the TV set was grand.
With satellite reception, they got movies on demand.
The speakers on the stereo played rap and rock 'n' roll,
since Harvey chose the music with his own remote control.

They had a full-time private chef, and every day he made
delicious pizza, burgers, ice cream, cake, and lemonade.
And on the roof they had a hoop for shooting basketballs.
There also was a swimming pool and even waterfalls.

His parents said, when all of them were finally inside,
"We'll travel 'round the country. We'll let nature be our guide."
But Harvey, who felt right at home, was having such a ball,
he said it wouldn't matter if they never left at all.

Neal Levin

Mom's Vacation

My mom took me out to the drive-in.
She took me to Zanzibar Lake.
We went to a reptile pavilion,
where we saw an enormous white snake.

She took me to play at the playground,
where we stayed all day long in the sun.
And even though I got a sunburn,
the pain was worth all of the fun.

We went to a dozen new movies.
I laughed till pop shot from my nose.
We stopped at a butterfly garden,
and one landed right on my toes.

We went for a ride on a ferry,
then went on a mountainous hike.
And then we went to a museum,
and we went for some rides on my bike.

My mom took me into the forest.
We camped out in spite of the rain.
My mom stubbed her toe on a boulder
and swore like a trucker from pain.

She took me to Animal Kingdom.
Then we went to the new public pool.
My mother can't wait till September
for a rest when I go back to school.

Kathy Kenney-Marshall

Farm Work, Not Homework

I have to work this summer
for my uncle on his farm.
The rooster crows at dawn;
I won't be needing an alarm.

I'll spend my days bent over
mucking out the chicken coop,
and nights telling Aunt Rhody
I don't want her chicken soup.

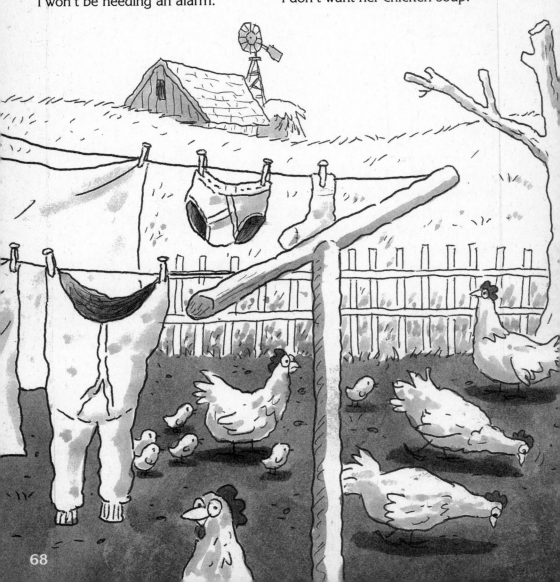

They don't own a computer.
I'll mostly be alone.
There is no cable TV,
and they only have one phone.

I'll put up with these problems.
In fact, I hardly mind.
As long as there's no homework,
I'll get along just fine.

Timothy Tocher

69

Welcome Back to School

"Dear students, the summer has ended.
The school year at last has begun.
But this year is totally different.
I promise we'll only have fun.

"We won't study any mathematics,
and recess will last all day long.
Instead of the Pledge of Allegiance,
we'll belt out a rock 'n' roll song.

"We'll only play games in the classroom.
You're welcome to bring in your toys.
It's okay to run in the hallways.
It's great if you make lots of noise.

"Your video games are your homework.
You'll have to watch lots of TV.
For field trips we'll go to the movies
and get lots of candy for free.

"The lunchroom will only serve chocolate
and Triple-Fudge Sundaes Supreme."
Yes, that's what I heard from my teacher
before I woke up from my dream.

Kenn Nesbitt

The Last Day of Summer

The last day of summer
is always a bummer!

Darren Sardelli

Credits

Author Index

Title Index